THE SMOKIES YUKKY BOOK

Horrifyingly true tales of our local flora and fauna

by Doris Gove
and Lisa Horstman

CONTENTS

Welcome to Your Nightmares

MORE CONTENTS

Your nightmare isn't over yet...

SECTION THREE

A face that sinks a thousand ships

SECTION FOUR

White Fang, Jaws, and The Sting
(but we ain't talkin' movies here...)

SECTION FIVE

Just plain creepy, alright?

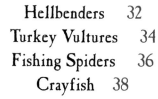

© 2006 Great Smoky Mountains Association
Edited by Steve Kemp and Kent Cave
Design by Lisa Horstman
Printed in China

4 5 6 7 8 9

ISBN 0-937207-48-9

GREAT SMOKY MOUNTAINS
ASSOCIATION

Great Smoky Mountains Association is a nonprofit
organization which supports the educational, scientific, and
historical programs of Great Smoky Mountains National
Park. Our publications are an educational service intended
to enhance the public's understanding and enjoyment of
the national park. If you would like to know more about our
publications, memberships, and projects, please contact:

Great Smoky Mountains Association
115 Park Headquarters Road
Gatlinburg, TN 37738 • (865) 436-7318
www.SmokiesInformation.org

Photo credits: Pat and Chuck Blackley, p. 58;
Rick Brown, p. 34; Michael Collier, p. 62;
Dave Haas/The Image Finders, p. 38; Bill Lea, p. 12 (left),24,
26, 28; David Liebman, p. 12, 14, 52, 54, 60;
Les McGlasson, p. 16; Don McGowan, p. 20, 22;
Joel Sartore, p. 8; A. B. Sheldon, p. 14 (right), 32, 36, 42,
44, 46, 48, 50; Gerald Tang, p. 10.

This book is for Andrew.
-DG

This book is for Dave in all his yukkiness.
-LH

WELCOME TO YOUR NIGHTMARES

Step inside...if you dare!

We are not making any of this up. WE ARE NOT! The stories here are true and come from studies by biologists and naturalists who love Great Smoky Mountains National Park. This book will help you recognize some things you'll see, such as poison ivy, Turkey Vultures, and bats. Maybe a yellow-jacket. Others you probably won't ever see—the snot otter, scorpions, a wood roach. But you will know THEY ARE HERE, watching you as you swim in the Little River and listening to your footsteps on the trail...

All forms of life in national parks are protected. You may not hurt, feed, pester, or kill them.

Question: "Does that include yellow jackets?"

Answer: Yep. But the rangers probably won't arrest you for self defense.

Question: "Can I give the bear a potato chip?"

Answer: No. Bears are wild animals.

If people feed them, somebody's going to get hurt, and it will probably be the bear.

Every living thing needs food, shelter, clean air and water, a way to defend itself and to reproduce. To us, the way they live might seem weird (a rattlesnake poisoning a mouse, a wasp paralyzing a spider) or unfair (cowbirds laying their eggs in other birds' nests). But hey, what would they think of us—grinding up cows to eat, driving around in huge polluting machines, fighting with each other to put a ball in a basket?

We hope this book will help you enjoy your visit to the Smokies. Remember, most of this stuff doesn't hurt people, so you shouldn't be afraid. But a few things could, so pay attention. Thank your lucky stars you weren't born a spider. And welcome to the real world.

Mwahahahahahahahahahaha

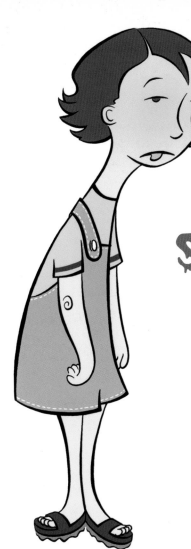

SECTION ONE
BLECH! Out-and-out disgusting

hahahahahahahahahahahahahaaaaaa!

CARRION BEETLES

Was it something I ate?

You're hiking along and see a dead bird or mouse near the trail. You lean over for a closer look...and it moves! Toward your foot! Its belly ripples as if there's a fight going on inside, but its legs are still and its head looks squashed.

Before you run screaming down the trail (you're not afraid of bird ghosts, ARE you?) nudge the corpse gently with a stick. Two or three handsome black and orange beetles may scurry out and run for cover under leaves. These are carrion beetles, also called burying beetles. Carrion (dead animals) is their favorite food.

When an animal dies, it gives off odors that alert flies, carrion beetles, and other scavengers. Often flies get there first and lay eggs (or in some cases, live, wriggling maggots) in body openings. Then a carrion beetle will fly in and establish ownership in the hopes that another of the opposite sex will show up soon. If more beetles show up, they will either fight over the prize or somehow split it. When a male and female meet over a carcass, it's love at first sight.

☞ NOTE TO THE UNAWARE

Dung beetles, relatives of carrion beetles, also live in the Smokies. Instead of dead bodies, they collect dung (animal droppings) and roll it into balls to bury for food for the whole family. So the environment has full-service clean-up—one beetle to pick up after animals that poop and another to drag their dead bodies away.

and then the cake? When carrion beetles or dung beetles find extra fresh..."stuff," first they suck out the delicious warm juice.

First they drag the body to a place with soft dirt. Then they dig underneath until the body slides down into the hole for storage. They pull the feathers or fur off and form the rest of the..."stuff" into a ball. They eat any fly eggs or maggots, and they may smear antibiotics from their spit on the ball to keep bacteria from growing on it.

Finally, they cover the ball with dirt and walk around on top to stamp the earth smooth.

It's a pretty weird lifestyle; maybe you SHOULD run screaming down the trail!

And by the way...

Sometime during all this work, the male and female beetles mate. The female lays up to 30 eggs in the dirt; when the larvae hatch, the parents and the delicious smell direct them to the ball of... "stuff." At first, the parents chew bits of meat to make baby food. The larvae stand up and beg by waving their front legs.

BROWN-HEADED COWBIRDS

Sheesh! What a moocher!

Under cover of camouflage, a female cowbird hops among the branches near a robin's nest. She lands on the edge of the nest, plops down inside, and quickly lays a speckled egg among the blue robin eggs. Then she flies away to join her mate on the lawn.

The robins return. "Hah!" they say. "It's the old cowbird trick." They manage to shove the cowbird egg out of the nest, and it splatters on the ground.

Not far away, a song sparrow sits on its nest trying to warm all the eggs—not so easy, because a cowbird has visited this nest, too, and its egg is larger than the other three.

The cowbird chick hatches first. It has a bigger mouth and a louder 'feed me' squawk than its three nestmates. Mama and Papa sparrow rush around to find juicy bugs, but Big Mouth gets most of the food. Two of the baby sparrows starve to death. Mama and Papa hurry to feed one baby that is bigger than themselves (the cowbird) and one little sparrow that never gets its share.

Cowbirds don't build nests or raise their own young—they borrow (or parasitize) the nests of other birds. They lay their eggs in the nests of other species because they never stay in one place very long.

When a cowbird sneaks an egg into a nest, some birds notice the new egg and either push it out, as the robins did, or abandon the

NOTE TO THE UNAWARE

Long ago, cowbirds followed buffalo herds across the prairies eating the bugs and seeds the big animals scattered. Because they were always on the move, they couldn't stop to build nests or raise young.

nest and build another one. Other birds see the cowbird egg and build a new floor in their nest, leaving the cowbird egg in the basement.

But if birds incubate a cowbird egg along with their own, they seem to have such a strong instinct to feed any open mouth that they just go ahead and take care of the big moocher.

WELL, HAROLD, I SEE THAT COUSIN OF YOURS STOPPED BY AGAIN.

AND SHE LEFT HER KIDS! THE NERVE!

And by the way...

Cowbirds can be seen around Sugarlands Visitor Center, Cades Cove, and other open areas of the park. Males have shiny black bodies and brown heads. If you see a couple of males, watch carefully for a camouflaged brown female that makes a quick visit and then flies off on another secret mission.

SCREECH OWLS

Tonight's menu special:
Fillet of hairball

This robin-sized owl doesn't screech at all. On the contrary, it has two rather pleasant calls. One starts high and goes down, like the neigh of a horse: OO hoo hoo hoo hoo hoo hoohoohoo
The screech owl's other song is a musical purr:

oo hoo hoo hoohoohoo

Screech owls own large territories so they can find enough food. They advertise their ownership by singing. Often when one calls, its neighbors answer.

Now we're going to HAVE to talk about owl hairballs. When a screech owl kills a mouse, it doesn't have a lot of time to waste on digestion. Being warm-blooded, it needs the food right away. And it needs to fly to catch more prey. It can't fly with a lot of extra baggage weighing it down.

NOTE TO THE UNAWARE

If you get hit on the head by a fresh owl pellet and you see several owl pellets on the ground, you're right under an owl's favorite resting tree. The screech owl is up there on a branch, but it camouflages itself by stretching its body up so it looks like a branch stub instead of a little round owl. It closes its eyes to narrow slits and watches to make sure you don't catch onto its trick.

SHEESH! AND I THOUGHT *MY* HAIRBALLS WERE NASTY!

So the owl swallows the mouse. The gizzard grinds it up and sends the meat and guts to the intestine and sends the hair and bone back up the esophagus, where it gets scrunched into a yucky hairy ball called a pellet. It has to get rid of the pellet before the next night's hunting, so it scrinches its eyes shut, opens its mouth, and, with a big 'GAAACK,' pops the spit-covered pellet out.

GAAACK!

AW, SHADDUP!

SCREECH OWLS

hair or feathers on the outside and bones on the inside, except that the bones are all mixed up. If you break a pellet open, you'll find tiny skulls, teeth, and leg bones. Really.

And by the way...
Owl eyes are so big they almost fill their heads, and they can't move their eyeballs in the sockets. They have to turn their heads to look around. They can turn their heads to see backwards (no, they can't keep going and spin their heads all the way around). To see better, they might also turn their heads completely sideways, so one eye is directly above the other. Do try this at home: move your head to see different things without moving your eyeballs.

WOOD ROACHES

These guys get plenty of fiber

It looks like a roach. It scampers like a roach. It IS a roach. A wood roach, that is, one of the fine upstanding citizens of a healthy forest.

Wood roaches live in rotting logs and show strong family values. A male and female live together for years and raise several broods of young. They build nurseries, hallways, and galleries in their log homes, then eat the walls. Both father and mother take care of the kids, and their main parenting job is...well, if you REALLY want to know, read on.

Wood roaches chew up wood, but they can't digest it. They have microscopic single-celled wiggly slimy helpers called protozoa in their intestines. The protozoa can digest wood, but they can't chew it up. So roaches and intestinal protozoa live together and need each other—a cooperative effort called symbiosis.

Here's the good part. Baby wood roaches need intestinal protozoa too. And where better to get it than from eating their parents' poop?

As soon as the babies have their own protozoa, the parents chew wood to a pulp and feed them...parental duties come from both ends. As they grow, young wood roaches get strong enough to chew their own wood.

Wood roaches help to rot, or decompose, the wood and return it to the soil so other plants can use the nutrients. The world just wouldn't work without them.

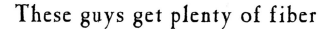

NOTE TO THE UNAWARE

Wood roaches can only live in healthy, old forests like the ones found in many parts of the Smokies. Forests where the trees are cut and hauled away for wood and paper don't have the rotting logs that roaches need.

roaches shed their skins as they grow. They also shed the lining of their intestines and all those friendly protozoa. Where do you suppose they get a new supply?

And by the way...

If you turn a mossy log over gently, you might see a wood roach family. The young ones, colored creamy white or light brown, usually scurry away first. Then the big shiny adults follow them. You can visit the same family day after day as long as you don't disturb the log too much or make it dry out underneath.

SLIME MOLDS

You've been slimed!

Nine or ten million people visit the Smokies every year. Some want to see bears or elk or scenery, but one group of Smokies visitors come just to study slime molds. Slime molds? You heard me.

In the first place, slime molds live a weird life. Most of the time they live as microscopic single cells, sliming along, eating bacteria and helping to break down leaves and other dead stuff.

Then something happens. These tiny cells search for each other and join up to become giant, slimy blobs that move by flowing in one direction and then in another. (In this case, "giant" means big enough to see, and sometimes as big as a dinner plate.) After a while, the blobs grow little knobs that look like tiny mushrooms. These release clouds of invisible spores that float on the wind and land somewhere to grow into new slime molds. (You might be breathing some in right now. HAHAHAHA! HEEHEE-HEEHEE!)

The second reason slime mold biologists come here is that so many different kinds of slime molds live here, and by studying them they can learn how the forest works and also how cells work. And slime molds move like animals and reproduce like fungi. Most living things do one or the other, not both.

When slime molds are in the big, visible blobs, they roll along eating everything in their path. They're too small to make great horror movies, but who knows? Maybe if all the slime molds in the park got together and came sliming down the mountains toward Gatlinburg...

NOTE TO THE UNAWARE

Some kinds look and feel like orange or yellow Cool Whip. Others look like sea foam flowing down a log. Some live on the ground and some in the tops of trees. In other words, they are all around you, whether you can see them or not...and whether you like it or not.

> PSSSST!
> HEY, KID—C'MERE!
> I WANNA TELL
> YOU SOMETHIN'.
> HEH HEH HEH HEH HEH...

[
And by the way...
If you see something that looks like the pictures of slime molds here, touch it gently with one finger. If it's soft and slimy, it may be a slime mold; if it's harder and smooth, it's probably a fungus. Wipe your finger on your socks. Or chase your little brother or sister with it.
Or your mom.
]

=POKE=

POISON IVY

Welcome to the Itchy and Scratchy show

Here's the weird thing about poison ivy: only people get it. Deer, goats, cattle, and rabbits eat it. Mice and rats can build nests in it. Caterpillars munch it. Birds eat the fruit and then scatter the seeds in their poop, which explains why poison ivy pops up everywhere.

It lives in the Smokies, and you have to watch out for it. You've heard "Leaves of three, let it be." There are other plants that have three leaves, but to play it safe—don't touch any of them until you really know. But the problem usually comes when the leaves, twigs, or stems (which are vines that look like hairy orangutan arms on the trunks of trees) touch YOU.

If you brush against poison ivy, a tiny bit of sticky, yellow oil gets on your skin. If it stays for more than five minutes, it can seep inside and introduce itself to your blood cells. Blood cells don't like strangers, and poison ivy oil makes them fighting mad—so mad that they destroy the oil and keep on fighting. This is called an immune response, and when you're scratching a few days later, the oil is long gone. So you can't give the poison ivy to anyone else, and if it spreads around your body, it is the immune response spreading, not the oil.

☞ NOTE TO THE UNAWARE

Biologists think poison ivy makes the oil to seal its own wounds or prevent bacterial infections (plants catch diseases, too), not to make us itch. It may be a coincidence that some people are so allergic to the oil...but on the other hand, maybe poison ivy just wants you to remember your trip.

20

HORRIFYING FAST FACT: If you know you've touched poison ivy, washing with non-oily soap such as dish detergent within a few minutes will help (though that's usually not possible out on a hike).

LOOK! FRESH MEAT!

LEG! MY FAVORITE!

OOOH, LOOK! ELBOW!

And by the way...

In the Smokies, poison ivy doesn't grow at high elevations or in shady woods. You'll find it mainly along roads and streams and in other open areas. To avoid poison ivy, stay on the trail and learn how to recognize the leaves so they can't reach out and touch you.

STINGING WOOD NETTLES

Don't tread on me

Some plants are hard to recognize, but stinging wood nettles have a way of introducing themselves that you won't forget. Like hikers, nettles love Smokies trails. They grow along the sides and lean toward the middle. From the top they look innocent enough...even pretty. But underneath the leaves and on the stems are tiny hairs. You have to look close, but not TOO close. Use a stick to lift a leaf, or very carefully grab the tip end of a leaf between finger and thumb and lift it to look at the underside.

When your bare legs brush against wood nettles, those hairs break off and slice into your tender skin. They carry a mixture of acids and other nasty chemicals. In about five seconds you feel a tickle, then a scratchy feeling, and then the full burn. As you rub, (which doesn't help) red bumps appear on your skin...you yell and jump around...right into the next nettles.

Raw nettles sting like crazy, but cooked? Mmmmm! They're nutritious, too—full of proteins and minerals. People use gloves or plastic bags to pick young nettles and then boil them to

NOTE TO THE UNAWARE

Baking soda breaks down the acid if you rub it on your skin right away. If you didn't happen to bring any, try human spit. The leaves of a plant that usually grows near nettles, called jewelweed, can relieve the stinging. But make sure you can tell jewelweed from nettles and poison ivy! With or without spit or other stuff, nettle stinging goes away in a minute or two (it only seems like forever).

break down the hairs and chemicals. You can find recipes for nettle soup, nettle pudding, nettle ravioli, and nettle root beer. It is said that eating this green food will shine your hair, clear your skin, and chase out any worms lurking in your intestines. Nettles may also help with colds and allergies.

LAW, EDNA! MY LEGS HAVE DONE BEEN SET AFIRE!

HEH HEH HEH!

[

And by the way...

One of the stinging chemicals is called formic acid. This is the same acid that you'd taste if you ate ants (not recommended, and besides, it's against the law to eat park wildlife).

]

23

SUNDEWS

Don't let the sunny name fool you...

"Come on over," it seems to purr. Little globs sparkle like jewels in the sun, and you just KNOW they're full of nectar—if you're a hungry fly, that is. You land on the ruby red leaf and take a sweet sip. Haw, haw! Joke's on you, bub! Your tongue geth thtuck. And a couple of legs! You jerk away, and the globs stretch like crazy glue...oops, there goes another two feet...and your thorax, your left antenna... oh no, your abdomen! Glue seeps into your breathing holes. As you suffocate, you think, "Hey, not fair. I'm an insect, and I'm supposed to eat plants, not the other way around."

Carnivorous sundew plants catch flies, gnats, mosquitoes, and other bugs. Globs on the tops of red hairs trap the insect, and then, in slow motion, other hairs with globs curve toward the prize and the whole leaf curls into a little bowl. The globs produce enzymes that digest the insect. Nutritious juice soaks into the leaf, leaving a little crumpled insect shell between the hairs. Then the leaf flattens out and makes new globs to attract the next unlucky bug.

Sundews and other carnivorous plants live in swampy places, where there is lots of water (enough for an endless supply of glue-globs) but not enough nutrients to make a living from dirt alone.

👉 NOTE TO THE UNAWARE

Sundew leaves make a powerful mix of chemicals: enzymes, antibiotics, a substance that can relieve whooping cough and asthma, and, of course, that stretchy glue. The enzyme that digests insects also curdles milk and has been used to make cheese. Venezuelan Beaver Cheese, anyone?

HORRIFYING FAST FACT: Remember those enzymes that digest insects? People used to use fresh sundew to cure warts—just slap a leaf on the wart and wait until it gets digested. Don't try this at home, please.

CAN I GET YOU A LITTLE DRINK, DEAR?

BWAHAHA HAHAHAHAHAHA HAHAHAHA!

[### And by the way...

At least two kinds of insects trick the trickster. Some ants snatch insects from the sundew leaves after the plant has gone to the trouble of catching them. And a kind of moth caterpillar eats the hairs, starting with the globs. Both the ants and the caterpillars have special hairs that don't stick to the glue.]

WILD HOGS

How to wear out a welcome

Here's the story of an alien invader.

Once upon a time (in 1912, actually), hunters brought 14 wild hogs from Russia to the mountains of North Carolina. They built a log fence around a big patch of woods and took good care of the hogs for ten years. By then, there were nearly 100 hogs, so the hunters went hunting.

The hogs didn't really care for the hunting part. They pulled a jailbreak, crashing through the fence and heading for the hills. They have been spreading through the mountains ever since.

The wild hogs are hairier and skinnier than farm pigs. They run fast, hide during the day, and stay together in family groups.

Wild hogs root in the dirt and eat flower bulbs and salamanders. After they've been through an area, it looks as if it has been plowed. They make muddy wallows and the mud washes into creeks. The hogs gobble up acorns and other foods that bears need to get fat for winter. And they carry diseases that humans and other animals can get.

Park rangers try to control the numbers of hogs by trapping and hunting, but nobody can get rid of them. They're smart and tricky and they like it here.

☞ NOTE TO THE UNAWARE

On the Appalachian Trail near Newfound Gap, park rangers have built a wire fence around an area full of wild-flowers. Hikers can cross the fence by walking up a grate, but hogs can't climb the grate with their pointy little hooves. Inside the fence, spring wildflowers grow like a carpet on the ground. Outside the fence, hogs have eaten the flowers and Roto-tilled the earth with their snouts.

as tusks and get sharp enough to slice someone's leg open. They usually run away, but don't approach or corner one.

LOOK, MA... IT'S...IT'S LIKE *OZ!*

HEAVEN'S GRATE
WILD HOGS PROHIBITED

GIMME!

GGAAAAAAR! MUST...EAT... PURTY FLOWERS...

And by the way...

One disease carried by wild hogs is caused by a slimy microscopic critter called Giardia that lives in hog guts. When hog poop washes into creeks, the Giardia goes with the flow. It can live in clear, cold water, and if you drink that water, you could get a case of diarrhea you wouldn't believe.

KUDZU

Jack's beanstalk

A snot otter might slime you. A screech owl might startle you at night. And there's a small chance that a rattlesnake will bite. But kudzu, an Asian plant in the bean family, sneaks up on you silently.

Green plants are good for us and for the environment, right? Well, listen to this story. A tree grows at the edge of the Smokies. Many kinds of trees, vines, flowers, and animals grow behind it. But in front, a dark green ocean zooms (in tree time) toward it, drowning everything in its way. Tiny tendrils reach toward the tree and wave around until they touch its trunk. Then they wrap around like constricting snakes and rush up, making big leaves along the way.

Kudzu leaves cover the tree's leaves, and, without sunlight, the tree starves to death. Then the tendrils reach out for the next trees.

👉 NOTE TO THE UNAWARE

You could call kudzu many names: Monster of the Woods...Green Hairy Octopus...Southern Strangler. But when people brought it to this country from Japan, they called it Miracle Vine and planted it in gardens (for its pretty flowers that smell like grape Kool-Aid), in pastures (for cattle feed), and along roadsides and railroads (to prevent erosion). It took people 100 years to realize that kudzu was a landscape-eating monster.

Insects and other wild animals that eat kudzu in Japan don't live here; that's why it's so out of control.

When you see kudzu by the side of the road, all you see is kudzu. No birds, live trees, or deer. You might see a mound of kudzu in the shape of a car or a house that it ate. Watch your back. And your car.

HORRIFYING FAST FACT: Kudzu may have 30 vines on one root, and each vine can grow about 60 feet a year. Some herbicides (plant-killing chemicals) just make it grow faster.

GEEZ, YOU LEAVE YOUR CAR FOR A FEW DAYS, AND THEN *THIS!*

HEY, LOOK, DAD! IT'S EVEN EATING THE *TIRES!*

And by the way...

This book includes two aliens. They didn't come on UFO airships—they came on regular ocean ships from other continents. These aliens are scary in a different way than the ones from outer space. For one thing, there's no doubt that they're real. For another thing, by the time biologists figure out what damage they cause, it's usually too late. Aliens have killed American chestnuts, elms, Fraser firs, hemlocks, and other trees. Other aliens, such as honeysuckle, take over places where native plants and animals should live.

SECTION THREE

A face that sinks a thousand ships

MIRRUH, MIRRUH,
ON DUH WALL,
WHO DUH MOST GOOD
LOOKIN' UVVEM ALL?
HUH?

HELLBENDERS

Fondly referred to as Snot Otters

Okay, so snot otter is just one nickname for the hellbender, North America's biggest salamander. Hellbenders live in clear, cool rivers like the ones that flow out of the Smokies. They are really, really slimy—slimy enough to make river otters gag and not want to eat them. The slime may also protect hellbenders from infection, because bacteria or parasites get caught in the snot.

A hellbender's body is flat, like roadkill, but its tail looks and works like a fish tail. Beady little eyes with no eyelids sit on the top of its head, and a flap of flabby skin along the sides ripples and waves in the current. Hellbenders have small gills and lungs, and the wrinkled folds of skin collect most of their oxygen.

Hellbenders are loners. Even when they get together in early fall for mating and egg-laying, they don't like each other much. A male digs a nest under a large rock, fights off other males, and then invites a female into the nest. She lays a string of yellowish eggs wrapped in jelly, and the male fertilizes them. As soon as they're finished, the male chases her out and tries to get another female. A large male may end up with eggs from several different females, and he guards them until they hatch about eight weeks later.

NOTE TO THE UNAWARE

You may never see a snot otter, though sometimes snorkelers catch a glimpse of one. But they're there, upstream from where you're swimming, lurking under large rocks, and oozing globs of slime into the water. Think twice before drinking out of a mountain stream, darlin'.

HORRIFYING FAST FACT: The most dangerous predators of hellbender eggs and larvae are...other hellbenders. There are no documented accounts of hellbender attacks on human beings, but there's a first time for everything!

Adult hellbenders may grow more than two feet long and may live up to 30 years. A Chinese hellbender relative gets five feet long and may weigh 100 pounds. That's a lot of snot.

*AW, BABY! YOU **KNOW** IT'S YOU I LOVE!*

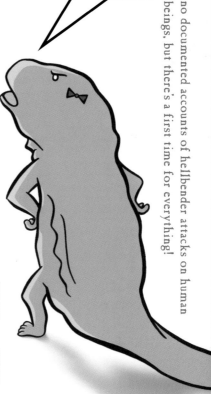

*DON'T YOU "AW, BABY" ME, YOU TWO-TIMING, CHEATING HEART, RAT-FINK **SNOT OTTER!***

And by the way...

Hellbenders eat crayfish, insects, worms, and small fish. They creep up on an unsuspecting victim and suddenly drop their lower jaw, sucking the food right in. If the prey is off to one side, the hellbender drops only the jawbone on that side; the other side of its mouth stays closed. Sharp teeth on the roof of the hellbender's mouth help hold the prey.

33

TURKEY VULTURES

A face only a mother could love

Such a pretty face: huge googly eyes, ear holes, hooked beak, wrinkled red skin with black fuzz patches, and see-through nostrils. Yes, it's true—if you look in one nostril, you can see right out the other side. These black birds, with six-foot wingspans, soar on masses of warm, rising air called thermals. It looks like fun, floating in the sky, wing feathers spread like fingers, no flapping necessary.

But it's work, too. From up there vultures look for dead animals or for other vultures that have already found one (vultures don't keep secrets very well). They can also smell the tiniest whiff of dead meat even if they can't see it from the air.

So why the naked head? Well, vultures do the big cleanup jobs—dead deer and such. To get the best parts, they reach waaaay inside...and sometimes it's pretty ripe in there. After a fine meal, vultures just give a good ear-cleaning shake to get the extra, uh, "stuff" off.

Vultures can digest disease germs and poisons that would kill most other carnivores. Their droppings are disease-free. Medical scientists would like to know how they do that. But we're not gettin' near 'em, thanks very much.

NOTE TO THE UNAWARE

Vultures can soar a mile high, or they can swoop below you when you stand on a mountaintop. They're mostly black, with some grey in the right light. They make no calls (they don't even have a voice box). As they soar, they rock slightly from one side to the other every few seconds. And they often soar in groups.

If you get too close to a cute, fuzzy little

vulture chick, you'll get a blast of vulture vomit in the face. Now THAT'S protecting yourself.

THAT'S IT, SON! BARF AT IT GOOD AND HARD!

I HEAR IT'S THE LATEST TECHNIQUE IN *PROJECTILE VOMITING.*

>GAK<

PROPERTY OF TURKEY VULTURE SELF-DEFENSE SCHOOL

And by the way...
Turkey vultures in the park often roost together in the same tree every night. While there, they spit up pellets of bone, hair, and other stuff they can't digest. In the morning they spread their wings to dry in the sun as they wait for thermals to form, so they can lift off for work.

FISHING SPIDERS

Shiver me timbers, mate!

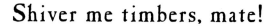

Spiders that catch fish?

Here's how they do it: They anchor two of their eight legs on dry land or a rock, stand on the water or leaves with four other legs, and hold the front pair of legs out and ready to pounce. Then they wait for ripples or vibrations on the water. When a fish or tadpole gets close enough, the spider lunges for it with fangs and front legs. Often the prey weighs much more than the spider, but she (sorry, guys, but it's the females that go fishing) pulls it out of the water with the help of those two anchor legs.

If the fish is out of reach, the spider wiggles her front feet in the water to send ripples like those that little bugs make. This may lure the fish closer. Fishing spiders eat insects, too, especially insects that fall on the water.

Fishing spiders can walk on water. Wax and little hairs on their feet hold them up; look for dimples on the water surface under the spider's feet. To go a little faster, the spider stands on four legs and rows with the other four. If it's breezy, a fishing spider can raise its body high on all legs and sail across the pond.

Fishing spiders can't dive, so if they need to hide under the water, they run down a stem or twig. By taking some air bubbles down with them, they can stay underwater for maybe 20 minutes.

 NOTE TO THE UNAWARE

Fishing spiders live on ponds or slow-moving sections of creeks. They hide if you move, but if you sit still, you might see one creep out and get into position. See if you can make the spider pounce by dropping an insect-sized bit of grass on the water in front of it.

Spiders paralyze their prey with venom and then add enzymes (digesting chemicals) to turn its body into a skin bag full of soup. Soup's on!

And by the way...
After mating, a female fishing spider makes an egg sack of web silk and carries it in her fangs. To keep from stumbling over it, she has to walk on tiptoe. If the egg sack gets dry, she dunks it in the water. Yes, like many other spiders, the female fishing spider eats the male after mating if he doesn't leave fast enough. After the spiderlings hatch, she builds a nursery web under leaves to protect them.

CRAYFISH

The handyman of creepy crawlers

A crayfish is like a Swiss Army knife. Wherever you look on its body you see some different kind of tool. In front, two long antennae wave back and forth—handy for feeling around in the dark. Then come little antennae with tufts of hairs that smell food. With eyeballs on stalks, crayfish see light and dark and sudden movements.

Short jointed legs surround the crayfish's mouth and push the food in as it's being chewed. (Imagine having fingers growing out of your cheeks to shovel in mac'n'cheese.)

Crayfish claws are like two different blades on the knife—one sharp enough to draw blood and the other strong enough to crush bones...well, fish bones anyway. But even a small crayfish can pinch hard.

Jointed walking legs move the crayfish forward. Some of the legs have little claws at the end that can pick up food (bits of dead fish, rotting leaves) and take them up to their teeth while the other legs keep walking. As they move, the legs make the feather-like gills wave about to get oxygen.

A crayfish tail has sections, a big strong muscle, and swim fins at the end.

NOTE TO THE UNAWARE

Crayfish break off their own claw or leg when a predator grabs it. They have a special muscle to break a joint, leaving the predator with a tiny snack, hardly worth the trouble. The crayfish can regrow lost claws, legs, or antennae, but they won't be as large as the original ones.

HORRIFYING FAST FACT: After shedding their shells, crayfish usually eat them. It's good recycling.

CRAYFISH

When you try to catch the crayfish, it whips the tail under its body and zooms backward into its hole, raising a cloud of mud. Under the tail there are little flippers, or swimmerets. So a crayfish can walk forward, swim forward, and dart backward.

Crayfish shells (or exoskeletons) cannot grow once they harden, so the crayfish must shed to grow. It sucks in water until it swells enough to split the shell right down the back. Then it pulls each leg, antenna, claw, swimmeret, eye stalk—very carefully—out of the old shell. The soft new shell hardens in a few days.

TOOL BELT? WHO NEEDS A *TOOL BELT?* I *SCOFF* AT YOU.

And by the way...

Some crayfish in the Smokies make chimneys near creeks. First they dig a tunnel, and when the tunnel is long enough that no predator can get them, they dig straight up. They crawl up the sides of the hole carrying lumps of mud to build up the chimney. When the mud hardens, it keeps the hole open so the crayfish gets oxygen.

SECTION FOUR

White Fang, Jaws, and The Sting

(but we ain't talkin' movies here...)

OH, YOU *ARE* BEING WATCHED, MY TENDER LITTLE MORSELS... YOU *ARE*!

TIMBER RATTLESNAKES

Watch where you step...or sit...or...

RRRRRRRRRRRRRRRRRRRRrrrrrrrrrrr...

It's coming from in front of you...a little to the left. So step back three giant steps and look around. Warn your companions. You might not see anything, but think 'camouflage' and look some more.

Timber rattlesnakes in the Smokies come in two colors: black and yellow. The fattest snakes in the park, they have a pattern of dark and light splotches along the back. Their heads are bigger than their necks since they make venom in their chubby cheeks. If the rattlesnake is coiled neatly in a sunny spot, leave the trail to walk around the snake from a distance of 20 feet or more. If the snake is crossing the trail, wait politely from a safe distance.

Rattlesnake venom can kill people, but they usually save the venom for its real job—to kill mice and rats. Millions of years before humans ever thought of it, venomous snakes developed hypodermic needles and use them, two at a time, to inject venom.

Rattlesnakes, whether coiled or straight, can strike faster than your eyes can follow the motion. But they can't jump or strike farther than half their body length, and they'd rather give warnings. Look at it from the rattlesnake's

NOTE TO THE UNAWARE

If someone gets bitten by a snake, the best thing is to stay calm and to get help from rangers or go to a hospital. Never cut the skin or apply a tourniquet. It might help to know that snake bites are rare in the Smokies and that no one has died in the park from bites by rattlesnakes or their cousins, copperheads.

point of view: It's dangerous to bite people, more dangerous to the snake than to the person.

Watch where you step or sit or poke your fingers. Rattlesnakes in the Smokies spend spring and fall in warm, rocky places. During hot summer days and nights they can roam anywhere in the park—any-where, that is, where there are juicy rats.

TIMBER RATTLESNAKES

paralyzes the rat so it can't breathe. The rest of the venom destroys blood and blood vessels so that by the time the rattlesnake tracks down the bitten rat, it is partly digested on the inside.

And by the way...
Timber rattlesnakes and copperheads, the only venomous snakes in the park, have small heat-sensing pits between the eyes and the nostrils. If you can see the pits, YOU'RE TOO CLOSE.

43

YELLOWJACKETS

Royalty runs an egg factory

"Hey, there's a big hole up there."

"Yeah, and there's a yellow cloud around it. I'll go check it...Yeeeowww! Ow! Run!"

It's September, and a ground-nesting yellowjacket nest might have 5,000 workers, along with hundreds of larvae and a food supply. Black bears dig the nests out to get those goodies; to bears, it's worth a couple of stings on the nose. After a bear leaves, the next lucky hikers get the blame.

Let's go back to the beginning. In April, a queen yellowjacket crawls out of a winter hiding place and looks for an underground home, maybe an old chipmunk hole. She gathers wood, chews it to pulp, makes paper cells, and lays eggs in them. She does everything herself, even though she's the queen. But when the larvae grow up, she sends them out to work. Then she stays home and lays eggs fulltime.

☞ NOTE TO THE UNAWARE

Some yellowjackets work as guards and stay near the nest. They sting anything that comes too close, shakes the ground, or touches the nest. Yellowjackets that you see in other places, such as picnic areas, won't sting unless you actually touch them. Don't slap at them or brush them off, and look before you lick your ice cream.

The workers use their stingers to paralyze prey—caterpillars, grasshoppers, maggots—and they tear flesh from dead animals. They deliver the food to the nest, and other workers chew it up to feed the larvae. Workers also snack on nectar, fermented wild grapes, ice cream, hotdogs, and lemonade. Workers, guards, queen...everybody in the nest is female, until the nights get cool in fall. Then the queen lays special, different eggs that will grow into males and future queens. These royal yellowjackets hatch, fly up in the air, and mate. Come winter, all the yellowjackets, except the mated queens, die.

animals in the Smokies. A single sting can kill a person who is allergic to the venom.

YELLOWJACKETS

PEEL ME A GRAPE, *BIG BOY.*

YES, M'LADY.

And by the way...
Yellowjacket guards tend to hang on tight
and sting several times. And while they're stinging
they release a chemical that works like a fire alarm—
when other guards smell it, they rush over to help.
Some crawl into hair or clothes. They can chase an
intruder at a speed of 6-7 miles per hour.
How fast can YOU run?

KINGSNAKES

The royal squeeze

You're a pretty little copperhead snake lying in warm sun. Little do you know that your worst nightmare creeps toward you...so slowly that you have no warning until you smell A KINGSNAKE! You jerk your head under one coil and try to hit the kingsnake on the nose with another coil. Somehow you know that there's no point in trying to bite—kingsnakes are immune to copperhead or rattlesnake venom. Too late. The kingsnake wraps around you, squeezes, grabs your head, and starts swallowing. You're lunch.

It takes a while for a kingsnake to push its food down to its stomach, inch by inch. And, since snakes are coldblooded, the copperhead doesn't suffocate as quickly as a mammal would. So the

👉 NOTE TO THE UNAWARE

Kingsnakes and ratsnakes rattle their tails if you come too close. It's a good trick, especially if the snake can rattle against dry leaves and grass. It fools some into thinking they're rattlesnakes.

PLEASE LEAVE.

copperhead's worst nightmare goes on...and on... probably even after digestion starts.

Kingsnakes flick their tongues up and down to smell their environment or to find food. But when they smell prey, they stalk the way a cat does, slowly and silently, and they only flick their tongues down at the ground so the prey won't see it.

Five kinds of kingsnakes live in the park. The most common ones are black, shiny, and have white speckles or narrow bands along their backs. They are very smooth and spend most of their time on the ground. Another black snake, the black ratsnake, often climbs trees.

HEY, BABY! WANNA BE MY *MAIN SQUEEZE?*

And by the way...

Kingsnakes, like other constrictors, lay eggs, usually under logs or rocks. The mother doesn't take care of the eggs. She just leaves, and the babies hatch about six weeks later. The babies have brighter colors and patterns than the adults, but they get darker each time they shed.
Some other snakes, such as copperheads, rattlesnakes, and gartersnakes, have live birth. The babies may stay with their mother for a few days.

KINGSNAKES

copperhead at the same time and both start swallowing, one from the head and one from the tail. When the two kingsnakes meet in the middle, the larger one just keeps going and swallows the copperhead and the other kingsnake! Really.

SNAPPING TURTLES

Touchy, touchy, touchy!

Hiss, lunge, snap, and stink—that's the snapping turtle motto. When cornered on land they stand as tall as they can on stubby legs and hiss. Since they can't see very well, they open their mouths and lunge, snapping at anything that gets in the way. Don't let it be your finger. The stink...Snapping turtles produce oily stuff that smells like rotten fish guts.

The top shell fits just fine and even has stylish knobs and points, but the bottom shell looks too small. Fat, flabby arms and legs bulge out, but don't be fooled. The flab covers strong muscles and sharp claws.

Snapping turtles spend most of their time prowling through mud, eating just about anything (including rotten fish guts) they can grab or tear with their strong jaws. They like fresh food, too. To catch fish, a snapper buries itself in mud except for its head. Then it opens its mouth wide and wiggles its little pink tongue, which looks just like a worm. And when a hungry fish comes...SNAP!

 ## NOTE TO THE UNAWARE

Like other reptiles, snapping turtles get their oxygen with lungs. They come to the surface to breathe through nostrils right at the end of their pointy snouts. If you're looking across a pond or swamp, you might see a little black snout; look for the dark shadow of the whole turtle underneath.

SNAPPING TURTLES

People have used snapping turtles to find drowned bodies: just tie some fishing line on the turtle and send it out in the lake.

And by the way...

Snapping turtles lay their eggs on dry land, sometimes far from water. The female crawls until she finds a place she likes, often an open area with soft soil. She uses her back legs to dig a surprisingly deep hole and then drops 20-40 ping-pong-ball-sized eggs into it. She scrapes the dirt back in the hole and packs it firm with her body. The hole is slanted, but even so, predators such as raccoons and possums may notice the disturbed dirt and find the eggs.

SCORPIONS

Devilishly romantic

Giggle! So romantic! During courtship, scorpions dance, holding hands...well, claws. They wind their tails together over their heads and dance, forward and back and sideways. No stepping on each other's toes, even though they have eight toes apiece. And sometimes (we are not making this up) they kiss.

The dance may look like a tug-of-war, but that's still the romantic part. Male scorpions put a little package of sperm on the ground and pull the female over it so she can pick it up and fertilize her eggs. Then he holds her claws really tight until he's ready to turn tail and dash to a hiding place. Even after all that romance, the female will eat him if he sticks around to chat. New moms have appetites!

A female scorpion can have 25-35 babies—live, squirming babies, not eggs. As they are born, she catches them by holding her claws like a basket, and then she uses her legs to boost them onto her back. They are soft and white, but their tiny stingers are ready to use. They ride on Mom's back for about ten days. She doesn't feed them—they have a supply of yolk in their bodies. When it runs out, they shed their skins, drop off, and set off on their own.

NOTE TO THE UNAWARE

The scorpions that live in the Smokies are small and light brown. They can't inject enough venom to be dangerous to people, but their sting can hurt (a little less on the pain scale than a bee sting). They live mostly in dry places with rocks and logs to hide under. You might see one by turning over a piece of bark, but be safe! Pull the far edge of the bark up so that the bark is between you and whatever's under there.

HORRIFYING FAST FACT: Baby scorpions are born live, each one
inside a tough little sac. They slice it open with their stingers to get out.

SCORPIONS

And by the way...

Scorpions don't chase their prey—they sit and wait.
Tiny hairs all over their bodies feel air vibrations when a
juicy cricket gets close. Then the scorpion leaps toward the prey
and grabs it with its claws. Unlike rattlesnakes and
spiders, scorpions don't use their venom to kill prey. It's for
defense only, especially against predators such as mice,
rats, and opossums. Their excellent sense of smell
tells them which prey is worth catching, and
female scorpions recognize their babies by smell;
they only let their own kids on board.

ANT LIONS

Room service, anyone?

Here you are, strolling along a nice sandy trail, minding your own business, *tra-la, tra-la*...when suddenly the sand gives way and you start to slide. No problem; you just shift to the other foot and pull away, but then *splat!*—a ball of sand hits you on the shoulder, and another on the knee, and then one right in the face. You grab at empty air, lose your balance, and start sliding, sliding, sliiiiddddddiiiinnnggg into a deep, dark pit, loose sand tumbling after you. You can't stop, and SOMETHING DOWN THERE IS WAITING FOR YOU.

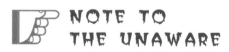

Well, you've just imagined the last day of an ant's life, the day it becomes lunch for an ant lion. An ant lion is an insect, and when it's still just a larva, it knows how to build a sneaky quicksand trap.

When the larva is hungry, it finds dry sand and crawls in a spiral, tossing sand out of the center with its flat head. It forms a cone-shaped pit and buries itself at the bottom with its curved, venomous jaws just out of sight. Then it waits. MWAA-HAHAHA!

Once the meal arrives, the ant lion grabs it, paralyzes it with one bite, and sucks out the juice. Then it flips the empty ant out beyond the edge of the pit and slips out of sight to wait for the next ant. Or caterpillar. Ant lions can capture prey bigger than themselves.

☞ NOTE TO THE UNAWARE

To see an ant lion larva, lean over its pit and stroke the sides of the pit gently with a pine needle. In the Smokies, look for ant lion pits at Alum Cave Bluffs or in shady, sandy places around old cabins.

HORRIFYING FAST FACT: Get this: an ant lion larva can't eliminate solid waste.

So as it eats and eats, it gets bigger and bigger until its abdomen gets round like a marble. When it's about half an inch across, it spins a silk cocoon and turns into a pupa.

And by the way...

Ant lions only poop once in their lifetime. Yep, it's true. After the pupa chews its way out of its cocoon, an opening forms at the end of the abdomen, and the ant lion produces a single pellet of waste. The opening closes and the ant lion (now skinny like a dragon fly) crawls out of the sand. It expands lacy wings and flutters up to hang underneath a leaf. They mate, the females lay their eggs, and after a few days, they die.

53

MUD-DAUBER WASPS

Martha Stewart can't top this one

When you visit an old cabin or barn in the Smokies, look for mud-dauber wasp nests on a rafter or wall. The nests look like small mud-colored organ pipes, usually five or six of them, about as long as cigars. The wasp that makes them is bluish-black with a skinny waist and a ridiculously small abdomen.

She makes the nest by scraping up mud from a nearby wet spot and carrying balls of it to her chosen place. Then she works it like clay to make a little mud room, lets it dry out, and closes it with a ceiling of mud. Ridges around the tubes show where she chewed the mud into shape.

Then the wasp flies out on a spider hunt. When she finds a nice juicy one, she lands on its back (so it can't bite her with its fangs), stings it a couple of times, and then curls her abdomen around and gives it a big sting in the stomach. This paralyzes the spider, but doesn't kill it.

But wait—there's more. She carries the spider back to a mud tube,

NOTE TO THE UNAWARE

Mud-dauber wasps live alone, not in hives as honey bees and yellow jackets do. That means that every female mud-dauber is a queen. They only sting spiders (but don't test this by trying to catch one).

There is another kind of mud-dauber that is a home wrecker. She finds an occupied organ-pipe nest, spits on the mud to soften it, then pulls out the egg and all the spiders. Next she goes about getting her own spiders and lays her egg on top. What a waste of good spiders!

chews open the ceiling, stuffs the spider in (by bonking it with her head), and goes after a couple more spiders. Then she lays an egg on top of the paralyzed spiders and makes a thick wall over the whole collection.

Whew! her work is done...but wait—there's another egg...and another, and so on, until she makes the four or five tubes, each one with several eggs lined up in private rooms—like a motel. Each room has wall-to-wall spiders. How's that for interior decoration?

EDNA! *GASP!* *LOVE* WHAT YOU'VE DONE WITH THE PLACE!

And by the way...

When a wasp larva hatches, there's its food: fresh paralyzed spider. At first the tiny larva sucks spider juice, but as it gets stronger it eats the spiders, legs and all. When the food is gone, the wasp larva spins a cocoon and changes into a wasp. It chews through the mud wall and flies away.
Thanks for the meal, Ma!

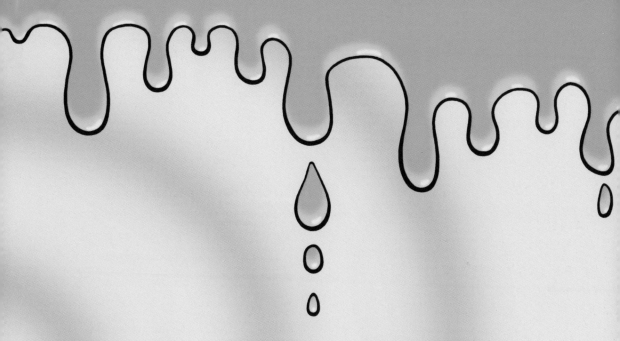

SECTION FIVE

Just plain creepy, alright?

LAUREL HELL

Get me outta here!

What's the most dangerous thing in the Smokies? Yellowjacket wasps? Rattlesnakes? Bears? Nope, getting lost kills more people than any animals. If you get off the trail—by accident or on purpose—you are in trouble. Big trouble.

Especially if you get off the trail and wander into a LAUREL HELL. These are areas where a variety of shrubs and other plants grow so close together it is almost like a spider's web. There is mountain laurel (sharp branches and twigs, tough as wire), rhododendron (thick twisty trunks like the arms of body-builders), greenbrier (thorny vines that grab a leg or neck and won't let go), doghobble (ankle and knee grabbers that even a dog can't run through), and camouflaged logs (usually about shin level, perfect to make you do a face plant). Some hells have witch hobble, too. It can trip a witch.

Mountain people call them laurel hells because you might never find your way out. You can crawl, push, thrash, and pull greenbriers off one leg just to feel them wrapping around your arm. Laurel grabs your collar. Doghobble clings to your ankles. Your sleeve snags on rhododendron. It's getting late. It's getting dark...

NOTE TO THE UNAWARE

If you do get lost in the Smokies, stop. Yell, blow a whistle, and stay in one place. There may be a laurel hell nearby just waiting to suck you in and close over your head. It's dark in there. You may never find your own way out.

LAUREL HELL

and you step on a rattlesnake that is resting beside a yellowjacket nest that happens to be between a mama bear and her three cubs. Ulp.

And by the way...
If you're a kid, somebody will come looking for you. If you stopped as soon as you noticed
you were off the trail, you have an excellent chance of
being rescued. But if you keep going, and you've
had the misfortune of entering a laurel hell,
it will probably be too late.

BATS

Did you hear that?

When you're 'it' in the game Marco-Polo, you close your eyes and yell "Marco," and the other players must reply "Polo," so you hear where they are to tag them. Bats do something similar called echolocation to catch things in the dark. They make high frequency (ultrasound) squeaks that are too high for humans to hear. The sound waves of the squeaks bounce off objects such as moths or mosquitoes or tree branches and travel back to the bat's ears.

Then the bat can change its flight path to either catch the insect or avoid the branch. Bats recognize each other by voice. When mother bats return home, where lots of hungry babies wait for them, they squeak. When their own babies answer, they fly to them and feed them milk. Then they wrap their wings around their babies and sleep. The next evening they hang their babies up by the toes and go out hunting again.

NOTE TO THE UNAWARE

Bats can catch an insect every two seconds and may eat 3,000 a night. They like mosquitoes. To catch prey, the bat locates it, dives toward it, scoops it out of the air in a basket formed by the webbing between its legs, reaches down with its mouth, eats it, and flies on—all faster than you can read this. With echolocation bats can even recognize what kind of insect it is, so they make sure to catch the tastiest ones.

Human brains make pictures from the light that comes into our eyes. Bat brains make pictures from sounds that come into their ears. Sonar copies bat echolocation to locate fish or the sunken Titanic. Medical machines use bat-like ultrasound echoes to make pictures of babies before they are born.

TRICKY TRICKY FAST FACT: Some moths escape bats because they can hear the echolocation sound waves and dive out of the way. It's the Marco-Polo strategy.

And by the way...
Several kinds of bats live in the Smokies,
(but sorry, no vampire bats here). Bats are the only
mammals that really fly, and their wings are made of thin skin
stretched between long fingers and toes. When the wings are open,
you can see blood flowing through tiny veins. There aren't many
caves in the Smokies, and conservation organizations have put
steel bars across some cave entrances to protect bats. If bats get
disturbed while hibernating, they may wake up and lose
some of the energy they need to last all winter.
If something scares a mother bat, she
may drop her baby.

MILLIPEDES

More legs than the Rockettes in a kick line

"How can you get around on all those legs without tripping?" an ant asked a millipede.

"Wow, I never thought about it before," said the millipede, tripping and falling flat on its face.

Millipedes, also called thousand-leggers, don't have 1,000 legs, but they do have a lot. Each of the segments (body parts divided by those lines that go across the back) has two pairs of legs. They crawl (when they don't have to think about it) by doing 'the Wave' with four or five groups of legs at a time. If you watch a millipede from the side, you can see the legs moving in waves.

Each segment does its own breathing through little holes on the bottom. All the segments share the same intestine, though, so like most animals, millipedes eat with their mouths and poop from their tails (one might be kind enough to demonstrate if you pick it up). Female millipedes lay eggs from segment #3, right behind their heads. Hatchling millipedes add legs and segments each time they shed their hard skins until they reach the adult number for their species.

NOTE TO THE UNAWARE

The biggest millipedes in the Smokies look like skinny brown sausages with waving antennae on the front end. In rain or wet weather, these millipedes climb the trunks of trees or crawl across the tops of stumps. Another, smaller kind of millipede has bright yellow or orange marks on each segment and smells like almonds if you pick it up. That smell comes from cyanide, a poison that can kill predators such as birds or mice. Most predators know that the bright colors are a warning about the poison.

TRICKY TRICKY FAST FACT: Millipedes make "unusual" nests—they eat dirt, digest the good parts, and poop out little balls that they shape into nests for themselves or their eggs.

MILLIPEDES

So how many legs? Well, count the segments, multiply by 4, subtract 8 because the first and last segments have no legs, then subtract 6 because segments 2-4 have 1 pair each, and then...oh, never mind.

SHOE SHOPPING? *AGAIN?*

And by the way...
Two groups of many-leggers live in the Smokies;
here's how we two-leggers can tell them apart:

Millipedes	Centipedes
· crawl slowly	· rush around like roller coasters
· curl up and produce stinky juice to defend themselves	· sting to defend themselves
· often appear out in the open	· stay out of sight under logs or rocks
· legs are underneath their bodies	· legs stick out on the sides
· eat rotting plant stuff	· eat meat (worms or bugs)
· don't bite or sting	· use venom for food-catching and defense, but Smokies centipedes are too small to sting a person